How to Start a Band

An Essential Guide to Starting a Band, Branding Your Style, Landing Gigs, and Attracting Fans

by Micah Nichol

Table of Contents

Introduction 1

Chapter 1: Finalizing the Talent 7

Chapter 2: Band Management Must Haves 13

Chapter 3: How to Land Live Gigs 19

Chapter 4: Other Paths to Fame and Fortune 25

Chapter 5: Branding the Band and Attracting Fans . 31

Conclusion 37

Introduction

Are you a talented musician who's looking to put together a band and — with any luck — rise to stardom, be paid to perform in front of a live audience, and even hear your music on the radio? Have you considered though that this effort is going to take more than just a group of musicians? While musicians often move people with their euphonious offerings, it's rare that they have a level-headed business mindset too, so for that reason it's critical to designate one person who can act as motivator, counselor, and business advisor all rolled into one. These functions are typically provided by a dedicated manager, who also acts as an accountant, a sales person and spokesperson, a public relations officer and legal aid, and whatever else the band may need them to be at the drop of a hat. Without the right person performing these functions, your band won't get much further than your parents' garage.

The good news is that, starting out, you can actually operate as your own band manager for a while. At least until your band becomes a household name and you can't even go to the grocery store without being asked for an autograph. No matter how hot your music is, the management of the band is what will ultimately determine your success.

While it's counter-intuitive, a band manager is just that — a manager. Like any office manager, your job isn't to juggle thirty roles at once and be mediocre at them all. It's to be great at one thing — finding the best ways to advance your band's name to fame. That also includes knowing when to search for people who can perform specific functions better than you. Your function is to serve as ringmaster of that crazy circus which forms part and parcel of a band's life — and do it so well that they can't function without you.

So if you're up for the challenge of wearing two hats — one as musician, and the other as manager — I encourage you to learn exactly what it takes to manage your band and actively seek out your band's popularity and financial success. This book is designed to teach you everything you need to know about putting together and managing a band.

© Copyright 2015 by Miafn LLC - All rights reserved.

This document is geared towards providing reliable information in regards to the topic and issue covered. The publication is sold with the idea that the publisher is not required to render accounting, officially permitted, or otherwise, qualified services. If advice is necessary, legal or professional, a practiced individual in the profession should be ordered.

- From a Declaration of Principles which was accepted and approved equally by a Committee of the American Bar Association and a Committee of Publishers and Associations.

In no way is it legal to reproduce, duplicate, or transmit any part of this document in either electronic means or in printed format. Recording of this publication is strictly prohibited and any storage of this document is not allowed unless with written permission from the publisher. All rights reserved.

The information provided herein is stated to be truthful and consistent, in that any liability, in terms of inattention or otherwise, by any usage or abuse of any policies, processes, or directions contained within is solely and completely the responsibility of the recipient reader. Under no circumstances will any legal responsibility or blame be held against the publisher for any reparation, damages, or monetary loss due to the information herein, either directly or indirectly.

Respective authors own all copyrights not held by the publisher.

The information herein is offered for informational purposes solely, and is universal as so. The presentation of the information is without contract or any type of guarantee assurance.

The trademarks that are used are without any consent, and the publication of the trademark is without permission or backing by the trademark owner. All trademarks and brands within this book are for clarifying purposes only and are the owned by the owners themselves, not affiliated with this document.

Chapter 1: Finalizing the Talent

Now, while some of you may be interested in becoming the manager of your *own* band, others of you may have sought out this guide purely to become a manager of someone else's band. That's fine too – this book is going to cover band management specifically, so just be sure to read it keeping your own scenario in mind.

If you're interested in managing your own band — effectively trying to serve as leader, manager, and alpha musician – eventually you're going to have to make the hard decision whether to be the musician or the manager. When your band becomes more successful, you'll need to split efforts: While the band spends hours on end playing and creating new music, the manager needs to spend every moment of that time *away* from them and concentrating on his/her own assigned responsibilities. The manager needs to spend every waking moment searching for new opportunities, while the band needs to spend those same moments raising their own bar so that people are more inclined to *give* them opportunities. And, once they *get* those opportunities, they need to *outperform* expectations so that others are even more inclined to give them a shot. No gig is simply a gig or a way to earn money; it's potentially another interview round for scouts who may give you the next big break.

But for now, when the band is just starting out, it's perfectly normal to serve as your own manager. You'll know when the time is right when you've simply become too busy to wear both hats. Whichever way you choose to go, for the remainder of this guide, I will continue to address matters with the implicit understanding that I'm addressing the **manager hat** that you're wearing, **_not_** the **musician hat**.

The next step which needs to be made is finalizing the talent—and this holds true even if you have a band already in place. The basic objective of a career in music is to devote all your dedication and efforts into making it to the big stage. This can't be achieved if two people in the band want to leave after a few years and pursue a career in law or accountancy, for example. While it may be prudent that everyone aiming to become a musician should have another professional back up to fall upon, there's no sense in planning the make-up of a band with failure in mind. Everyone in there should be determined to throw the rest of their life aside and devote themselves to their music at all costs. The last thing you need is for someone to walk away when all you needed was that last *final* push to eternal fame.

With this in mind, remember that immediate talent (while all-important) should take a slightly lower relevance as a selection criteria in comparison to the potential to get better, attitude towards cooperation, devotion to music and the band, and integrity of sound over money. So, if you have two choices for lead guitarist—one immensely talented player who is highly individualistic, and wants to join the music game to make money at any cost, and another who is slightly less talented, slightly more given to cooperation and collaboration, has time and dedication on his side which proves that he may get much better with time, and values the integrity of music over individual opportunity to make music, pick the second one.

Again, it's counter-intuitive, since bands often try to cram themselves with the most talented members right off the bat, even if they get along together as well as a pack of dogs quarrelling over the last morsel of food. The problem with that—even if this all-star band blows the competition out of the water as it rushes out of the gate—is that the members will most likely engage in egotistical battles soon after, give their individual needs greater priority over the needs of the band, and will likely split if they get better offers on their own, or from other bands.

Therefore, if you feel as if some members of the band do not have their music as their highest priority in life, or could likely change it to another profession in the near future, or seem to create friction within the group—it's best to weed them out. That may seem harsh, but sometimes hard decisions need to be made for the betterment of the group in the long term. You don't want the mediocre efforts of one or two people to negate the hardest efforts of the others.

You need to also keep in mind that this particular decision should not be taken by you as an individual, but rather should be explained to the group as a whole and decided upon together. As the manager, your job isn't to act as dictator, judge, jury, and executioner, but rather as a facilitator of difficult solutions. If the people to be weeded out have spent significant portions of their time and efforts in the past for the betterment of the group, assign them secondary positions within the band's brand as a whole—maybe taking their other talents into account. We've already discussed the higher criteria for selection of new members, if you find yourself faced with the need to hold auditions for replacements, and so you need to stick to those characteristics in such a situation.

Once your talent has been finalized, and the band has taken shape, be sure to assign equal positions within them (as best you can) to avoid future problems with each individual's sense of importance and contribution to the music as a whole. After they start practicing together, you need to keep an ear out to ensure that each member is contributing vital portions of their musical sensibilities to the sound of the band as a whole. Often, the *sound* of the band is determined by the music of the leader. The problem with that is that they represent a single over-riding influence from another band or musician—and the band's music as a whole comes off as derivative or repetitive rather than original or unique. No one ever got to the top of the charts by simply ripping off from other musicians, or playing cover songs alone.

Therefore, encourage each person within the band to try to alter their own contributions based on their individual influences as and where possible. In order to avoid the stamp of a single person or influence on the output, encourage as many of them to write their own lyrics or songs. This would provide you with a medley of music that showcases the breadth and depth of musical knowledge and influence of your *entire* band, thus increasing the chances of fans to connect with one or the other song in their final offerings. It will also reduce the chances of individual members splitting off in the future because they felt that their own voice was often ignored.

Chapter 2: Band Management Must Haves

As I mentioned in the beginning, the overriding quality of band managers is the ability to unearth and cement as many opportunities for their bands as possible. This requires a dedication and unending devotion to the success of the band that goes beyond paltry monetary concerns. If the band you work with is only interested in you for the amount of money you could possibly make for them, you (collectively) will likely never see the upper echelons of success. The best band managers who worked with just one band often reached their legendary levels of stardom because they worked their rear off with a passion for their chosen musicians. This passion didn't come from the money, though plenty of that saw its way to them soon enough, but rather because they wanted more and more people to hear the music that their band had to offer.

Therefore, the first great quality of band managers is that they absolutely love the music of the band. This may change as you make your own name in your own right and start taking on more customers as you touch success. But, as a starter, this single quality will determine the depth of your own sacrifices which will allow you to build a valuable network to launch future careers later on for the pure attraction of money. As a beginner manager, choose a band that you truly believe in, and your work will come a lot easier to you.

The next quality of band managers is that they are salespeople, first and foremost. Their scruples are limited to the way they treat their bands. But, beyond that, they aim to conquer any advantage that would give their bands the slightest fighting chance at stardom. They aren't afraid to reject, "No," as an answer, and to persevere till they've convinced others of the worth of their chosen music. They also aren't afraid to bluff if necessary, haggle upwards where they feel as if their band is getting less than its market worth, and to finagle creative deals with established people in the music industry which may offer something of value to both parties involved at the end of the day. Remember the pushy car salesman at your nearest auto dealership? Not the sleazy one, but the smart one who *actually* delivers sales. That's who you have to be all day every day.

However, to be able to dig up opportunities, you need to be in a position where you're *aware* of such opportunities as they present themselves. And for that, you need to stay well-connected with all levels of the music scene. So, the next quality of a manager is that they're extremely savvy at networking. Successful managers not only make use of their friend circles, but of subsequent acquaintances and other connections as well. They also keep themselves updated on the smallest details of the music industry around them—owners and various influential personalities within record companies, radio jockeys and music directors within radio stations, owners of fests and other establishments (resto-pubs, lounges with live bands, etc.) which regularly give new bands a chance at greater exposure, and even tournaments which may help your band show off its capabilities. Not only are great managers always aware of the state of the music industry at large, but they're intimately connected with the local music scene around them. Wherever they feel as if they're lacking sufficient connections, they actively seek out people who may help them penetrate the industry to greater effect.

Within the band itself, great managers aren't heavy handed, but rather seek to ease the frictions within the individual members. They also don't force their own opinions and beliefs upon the band members, but use their salesmanship to persuade the band to make better decisions. As such, they foster a harmonious environment which delivers greater results through collaboration, rather than create an atmosphere of conflict and competition within the band itself. They also recognize the importance of stable personal lives for musicians, and help smooth over the various ups and downs which come from having to devote significant parts of their collective lives in the pursuit of better music—often with little income or remuneration in the beginning. This is significantly harder than it seems to be at first glance, since various factors in a musician's life will often vie for professions with stable incomes for them.

When they need it, managers will also act as counselors and shoulders for the band members. However, as I've mentioned before, there is little sense in juggling hats which you know are beyond your capacity. Therefore, for each job, whether as a lawyer, psychiatrist, or even as a friend, if you think someone else close to the band can deliver a required result better—it's your job to convince and employ them for that purpose. In the end, you need to be accurate in the assessment of your own talents, and utilize help from your musician's networks wherever you feel that someone else can get results faster. As I mentioned, your ultimate responsibility is to be protector and ringmaster—shielding your musicians from the backlash of everyday life, managing their basic needs so that they can concentrate on making great music, and organizing the various forces at your disposal to give your musicians the best shot at making their name.

Chapter 3: How to Land Live Gigs

For a musician, the name of the game is exposure. There are thousands of great bands out there, and many of them are either just as good as or even better than your band. However, talent only plays a small part in the ultimate destiny of each musician. Those who are famous would tell you that their life, as it played out, did so through a convergence of six factors—hard work, sacrifice, ultimate determination, perseverance, preparation, and large doses of luck.

While most of the mediocre to great bands have the first five factors in common, the sixth one plays the largest part in deciding who gets forgotten, and who plays on the next great stage beside other established names. You never know if the guy sitting in the audience of your local club is a scout from a music company, or even the legal counselor for an event management organization. Therefore, you need to aim to be on as many stages, playing for as many audiences as you can. Yet, you need insider understanding of the industry to ascertain which bars, pubs, and stages get frequented more often by important people from the industry.

This last point is vital—participation in certain events, or playing at some establishments will inevitably stop you from gaining meaningful employment in the industry. You need to figure out which events and establishments embody this principle in your neighborhood—where music careers go to die—and turn such opportunities down, regardless of the dearth of jobs in such times.

When landing live gigs, the first thing that matters is the possible exposure of the band so far. Apart from providing great music which is in keeping with the sensibilities of the establishment, patrons also appreciate having familiar names play for them while they enjoy the services available to them. With that in mind, and to reduce the sensitivity to pressures upon musicians when performing live as an added bonus, you can perform a random street tour. If your city supports street music, and does not dissuade street performances, you could organize a day out for your band where you quickly set up and perform a few numbers at five or six different locations. These random street performances can be repeated a few times every week in order to increase the visibility of your profile among the inhabitants of your city.

Once your name recognition starts rising, approach the owners of establishments which support live bands and have helped launch musicians in the past. Take a video copy of the street performances with you, and use that material to pitch your band to the owners. Make sure to match the places you pick to the kind of music played by your band—you can't take the music reel of a rock band to a jazz club and expect that to work.

Once you've landed live gigs at reputable places, use the same accomplishment to land you further gigs at other spots. Send your music reel to event management companies which often handle concerts for larger bands, and personally approach their executives for a chance to open up for one of the main acts. At this point, the larger your public profile, the greater your chance of receiving a favorable answer. While the public street performances always carry an inherent risk of ridicule, the positive payoff is greater recognition from the everyday person—the consumer at the end. Also, if you can get one or two bylines in any newspaper at this point, covering your band's strange roving impromptu concerts, the exposure you receive is sure to gain you more opportunities as warm-up acts at large concerts.

Also, don't be ignorant enough to limit yourself geographically within your own city. If there are significant musical opportunities to be exploited in surrounding cities as well, take your band's music reels, videos of performances, list of past achievements, etc., and try to score further events and gigs through live-music establishments, event management companies, and so on, in those arenas as well. If you wish to launch your band on to the mainstream, you need to have a larger following than just the people of your own town. The closer you get to become a nationally known musical force within your country, the better your chances of receiving a company contract for your band.

Chapter 4: Other Paths to Fame and Fortune

The problem with most struggling musicians is that they narrow down their own acceptable ways to fame. They consider themselves as too important to play in certain events or have their music associated with specific sorts of endeavors, before even having made themselves into a vaguely recognizable name. The issue with that outlook is that it blocks many legitimate claims to fame which would have supplemented their existing and acceptable opportunities instead of having to struggle day in and day out while limiting themselves to a single and highly specific path to success. You need to remember that success is a numbers game—if a hundred opportunities are made available, maybe three of them would ultimately lead to grandeur and fame. However, if you limit yourself to capitalizing on fifteen out of those hundred doors, you risk cutting off the opportunities which would have launched your band onto the grand stage.

With that in mind, a manager needs to be creative enough to explore alternative paths to getting the band on the air. The most well-known one among them is contacting radio jockeys and stations to air music from your band. If this plays out well, it functions as an effective launch pad for musicians' careers. However, this approach requires great finesse, and is a test of a manager's networking and sales skills. Most radio jockeys often get dozens of music reels from struggling bands, all of which hope to be aired in the hopes of landing larger deals. Yet, radio jockeys can't stuff their airwaves with unknown music, or else their own audience numbers would suffer greatly. Therefore, radio jockeys only choose to air bands which suit their own personal musical sensibilities, as they aim to infuse their programs with the force of their own personalities and the stamp of their own tastes. Moreover, there are plenty others who may need something *extra,* without further expounding upon this, to choose one band over another.

So, when you intend to deal with opportunities on airwaves, try to create recognition in neighborhoods where you know Radio jockeys either frequent or reside. You can either use the street performances, or target live-band opportunities in such locales to increase your presence recognition. If you don't believe that any of these would help you against a particularly impervious radio jockey, you could also attempt to get onto the airwaves for the show by approaching the music director of the same. The music director, in most stations that have one, is responsible for compiling the music library based on increasing demand and for pulling and providing recommendations to jockeys in instances where they haven't explicitly given an entire program's worth of music in advance and so may have some free slots left. As opposed to radio jockeys, music directors are far less rigid with the specific tones and criteria for music selection in a program—though they're still quite stringent about quality. So, if your music's quality speaks for itself and you manage to secure a meeting with a music director, this may be your best way in for cases where the specific radio jockeys are difficult to approach.

Also, while working on opportunities for live gigs, create an entire album's worth of songs through the band. Once the band is entirely satisfied that this particular reel embodies the *best* of their abilities, hire a semi-professional recording studio which pays per hour, instead of per day. After the recording is complete, burn about thirty copies from the master record itself for best sound clarity.

With these copies in hand, revisit your previous research regarding the record companies and other echelons of the music business in your locale. Identify various medium to upper level executives across the board who may be interested in either hearing back from you, thanks to your previous efforts at networking, or who may be interested in backing the sound of your band onto larger markets. Although, if you intend to mail these copies in, you need to remain aware of one potential risk—intellectual property in matters of music is a murky field at best for those performers who don't gain instant recognition for their efforts. For the mid to lower level musicians, there isn't much of a protection against having their music or lyrics copied and exploited by companies through their established performers. Therefore, sending a copy in without adequate proof backing up your work carries large risks of intellectual exploitation.

Whether or not you decide to send your band's work to record executives, there are other avenues available for you to make ample use of these recordings with far less risk of your work being poached. For example, you could choose to send your band's music reel to various TV shows and ask them if they would like to use any of your music within their programs. To sweeten the deal, you could also offer them the use of one song without any royalty fees whatsoever, and any others at severely reduced royalty fees than the usual market rates. While this may represent some loss from a potential income source, their acceptance would launch you onto national (and potentially global) television, with all the exposure that it entails. In this day and age of hyper-active Googlephilia, it takes viewers about ten seconds to look up the provenance of particularly memorable music anyway, which then opens doors to further deals and gigs.

Moreover, with the increasing relevance of indie movies on the cinema circuit, you could also send music reels to the largest drama or videography departments on college circuits through the country. Similar to the deals made with TV shows, you could offer the use of one of your songs free of royalty. Though you should avoid signing any exclusivity deals, and should accompany the sample reel with strict legal contracts reducing the chances of intellectual infringement, exposure through an indie movie (particularly if you've done your homework, and are providing your music to a well-made one) is an awesome stage for exposure of your work.

Lastly, upload your album to websites such as CDBaby, Tunecore, Spotify, SoundCloud, iTunes etc. You can either choose to release specific singles for free and link people over to albums on sale on the other websites, or directly release some albums for free while releasing others on sale alone—whichever approach you may see fit. Not only do these websites free you from needing records and other companies to provide you with any fan base or exposure, they also allow you to assess your market worth in the opinions of listeners directly, and control your own pricing as you see fit.

Chapter 5: Branding the Band and Attracting Fans

Everything in this day and age is a brand—whether an individual, an organization, or even an abstract concept such as freedom. If you're confused about the last part, think about the extent to which the word "freedom" is associated with the United States, despite the fact that it isn't the only country in the world where the citizens enjoy their freedoms as guaranteed and upheld by law. *This* is the power of the brand. And brand value, along with brand recognition, makes or breaks bands today.

Before we delve deeper into this, I need to dispel one misconception—branding isn't just about pumping out clothing from a t-shirt cannon into an inebriated crowd. The purpose of building a brand is to consolidate your collective essences into a single, concentrated form which allows people to picture the musicians as a collaborative group by recalling their name alone. It also enables you to infuse the secondary and tertiary layers of a listener's recall with attributes that hold true for the collective, even if they aren't so for the individuals within the band. If that statement's obscure, it refers to the feelings and emotions generated within a listener or audience member when they recall your band. Do they think that the band makes amazing music? Is it lame or cool? Does it tug at their emotions, whether passion or rage? Is it symbolic of everything they love or hate within that particular genre of music? Do listeners find the performers deep, mysterious, gregarious, fun, or pretentious?

If you understand the depth of emotions which are associated with every loved and hated band among music lovers, you can begin to appreciate the complexities linked with proper brand building. And all of it starts with the name and logo.

While I don't need to explain this, the name of a band is its core identity. Once a name is publicized, it shall never change again for as long as that can be helped or maintained. Every effort in increasing the exposure of a band as a collective is made towards increasing the recognition of its *name* among listeners. And so, the name which is chosen should embody the attributes cherished by the members, and yet should be deeply memorable. Whether it's deep, sarcastic, funny, dark, or comical, the name should only be finalized through the consent of every member of the band *and* you, since you'll be working just as hard to increase the recognition of that chosen name. Standing behind them with all your passion and drive is only possible if you don't wince or groan inwardly every time you have to say the name of the band out loud.

Secondly, the logo of the band is another piece of its brand that never entirely changes. It may be slightly modified or nuanced from time to time, but it will never change in its entirety. Therefore, the usual recommendation is to get the logo made with as much thought as possible, and professionally if you can help it. If you can't get it made professionally at first, try to come up with a design together which all of you wouldn't mind living with till you can afford to get it re-done more professionally or in deeper detail—but the basic design still won't change.

Thirdly, you need to open up accounts under the name of your band on every social media platform. Additionally, create a website specifically for your band—containing profiles on the musicians, their past work if any, and shorts from any fest or other avenues where they may have played together. You can also create splash pages on this website to create a mailing list for fans, and you can keep them updated on further events and releases through mailer manager programs like MailChimp.

Furthermore, you can use websites like Spreadshirt to design and create different paraphernalia such as t-shirts, badges, patches, etc., for your performances, or on limited offer to fans with the purchase of CDs and other modes of distribution of your band's music.

Lastly, if you wish to preserve the integrity of your band's name and objectives, you can also retain autonomous power by starting campaigns on fan-funding sites such as PledgeMusic, ArtisteConnect, TuneFund, etc.

Conclusion

While being in a band means that you're often blissfully unaware of the depth and scope of your own problems, that's only because you have an extremely talented manager sweeping these problems out of your way before they can impede your progress.

That said, being a band manager is an extremely thankless job—often netting scorn without so much as a hint of gratitude from those whom you help launch. Not only will the ones you rocket to stardom rarely ever show you true displays of appreciation, unless you're lucky, you will also suffer from rocky personal relationships for several years since you'll have to devote most of your time to being on the road in search of opportunities. This is why this position isn't for those who think they can reach the pinnacles of managerial success in this field by treating it as a part-time gig. Also, while you're busy breaking your derrière for your musicians and traveling up and down the length and breadth of the surrounding cities, scouring for gigs and chances, you will also have to keep yourself in tune and up to date with any happening of note within the local music scenes of the cities which you target.

While the new digital age has made life much easier for band managers by reducing the dependence on large companies, and by linking musicians directly with fans for financial independence, it has also increased the complexities involved in securing the intellectual property rights of your musicians' work. Furthermore, with the rising levels of internet piracy, it has become far more difficult for smaller bands to be properly compensated for their hard work and effort. Therefore, although a manager's job may be easier in some aspects, it has become far more convoluted in others—especially since bands with some experience now tend to operate without managers altogether, believing themselves to be more than capable of interacting with fans directly to bring their joint dreams to fruition.

However, as you may have understood by now, this isn't a job for the faint of heart. Regardless of whether you manage to find the best employees to serve other functions, you need to function as a talented negotiator, tech-savvy maestro of logistics, peacekeeper extraordinaire, and a creative accountant who excels at efficiently marshalling resources at the very least. But, no matter what, I can guarantee one thing—the phase of life you're about to enter will be the most fun you'll ever have.

Finally, I'd like to thank you for purchasing this book! If you enjoyed it or found it helpful, I'd greatly appreciate it if you'd take a moment to leave a review on Amazon. Thank you!

Printed in Great Britain
by Amazon